The Christmas Story

JIM AND BONNIE INKSTER

SM**5**TH
S T O N E S

Kelowna, BC
Canada

DEDICATION

We dedicate this book to all those who are seeking the Father as Jesus said in John 4:23: "Yet a time is coming and has now come when the true worshipers will worship the Father in spirit and truth, for they are the kind of worshipers the Father seeks".

CONTENTS

ACKNOWLEDGMENTS

Scriptures taken from the Holy Bible, New International Version®, NIV®. Copyright © 1973, 1978, 1984, 2011 by Biblica, Inc.™ Used by permission of Zondervan. All rights reserved worldwide. www.zondervan.com The "NIV" and "New International Version" are trademarks registered in the United States Patent and Trademark Office by Biblica, Inc.™

The Christmas Story

Jim and Bonnie Inkster

1 THE CHRISTMAS STORY

At Christmas Bonnie and I traditionally read His story. We read it every year on the 25th from Luke. Why? Well, Luke is the gospel that seems to have all the elements in keeping with our modern celebration of that event. As we looked into the first three chapters of Luke I thought I'd check out Matthew. The impression that grabbed me was Luke seems to be written from Mary's perspective and Matthew seems to be written from Joseph's perspective. In keeping with that impression Bonnie has written on Luke and I wrote on Matthew. We hope that you will enjoy our thoughts on the Christmas story.

As I read through the accounts I was impressed with how much the whole event of Jesus' conception and birth does not resemble our celebrations. We have sanitized and fantasized what was really a time fraught with danger and shame, but amazingly great courage. Over the years of reading the gospels Joseph has gone from being almost a nonentity in the whole situation to being one of my heroes of faith. I will expand on that as we go through the events surrounding the birth of the Son of God.

Keep in mind that scriptures tell us in Galatians 4:4 "But when the fullness of the time had come, God sent forth His Son, born of a woman, born under the law". This was the culmination of prophecy and long awaited expectation. The fullness of time is key. There is no mistake about the point in the history of man when He appeared. The people involved were not randomly chosen but vital personalities in the completion of redemption. This was not a cool, frost laden evening that was fantasized. This was a culmination of time – fullness - when everything was complete.

It happened over a period of at least three years. Elizabeth was pregnant for 6 months before Mary. The wise men arrived possibly up to 2 years after Christ's birth. The events were so spaced out that one would easily miss the significance of this birth. Bethlehem did not have a strip like Las Vegas all lit up in neon with signs pointing to the stable. The inn was not inundated with shepherds, wise men, town's people and little drummer boys on the evening of His birth. The shepherds, who had a visitation of angels, came to the inn, saw the baby as they were told, and did tell people in the hill country what they had experienced. No one else seemed to venture to the stable at that time. Neither Herod, the king, nor the people's chief priest nor the teachers of the law were aware of any unusual event. Only the enquiries of the wise men drew any further attention at a national level to the blessed event.

How significant is the pattern we see here? God seems to enjoy changing the world through small beginnings. He starts with an insignificant person, infuses them with His love, His spirit, and they leave a mark that indelibly stamps the history of mankind forever. Look at the men of God and their meager beginnings. Abraham was one of three sons, not even the first born, with a barren wife. God made him into a Father of many. David was the youngest of his family, not even fit by his father's estimation to be brought before the prophet, Samuel. Joseph, a carpenter, became the legal guardian of Jesus, the Son of God. Jesus, born in a stable, a simple carpenter from Nazareth, a town of no reputation, brought us the greatest gift the world will ever experience.

As we ponder the goodness of God to mankind this Christmas ask yourself the question 'what about me?' What could He do with me? What would He ask of me? Would it be anything more than 'be obedient' to the call He has placed on your life? Come follow me.

2 THE SCRIPTURAL ACCOUNT ACCORDING TO MATTHEW

Chapter One

1 A record of the genealogy of Jesus Christ the son of David, the son of Abraham: 2 Abraham was the father of Isaac, Isaac the father of Jacob, Jacob the father of Judah and his brothers, 3 Judah the father of Perez and Zerah, whose mother was Tamar, Perez the father of Hezron, Hezron the father of Ram, 4 Ram the father of Amminadab, Amminadab the father of Nahshon, Nahshon the father of Salmon, 5 Salmon the father of Boaz, whose mother was Rahab, Boaz the father of Obed, whose mother was Ruth, Obed the father of Jesse, 6 and Jesse the father of King David. David was the father of Solomon, whose mother had been Uriah's wife, 7 Solomon the father of Rehoboam, Rehoboam the father of Abijah, Abijah the father of Asa, 8 Asa the father of Jehoshaphat,

Jehoshaphat the father of Jehoram, Jehoram the father of Uzziah, 9 Uzziah the father of Jotham, Jotham the father of Ahaz, Ahaz the father of Hezekiah, 10 Hezekiah the father of Manasseh, Manasseh the father of Amon, Amon the father of Josiah, 11 and Josiah the father of Jeconiah and his brothers at the time of the exile to Babylon. 12 After the exile to Babylon: Jeconiah was the father of Shealtiel, Shealtiel the father of Zerubbabel, 13 Zerubbabel the father of Abiud, Abiud the father of Eliakim, Eliakim the father of Azor, 14 Azor the father of Zadok, Zadok the father of Akim, Akim the father of Eliud, 15 Eliud the father of Eleazar, Eleazar the father of Matthan, Matthan the father of Jacob, 16 and Jacob the father of Joseph, the husband of Mary, of whom was born Jesus, who is called Christ. 17 Thus there were fourteen generations in all from Abraham to David, fourteen from David to the exile to Babylon, and fourteen from the exile to the Christ. 18 This is how the birth of Jesus Christ came about: His mother Mary was pledged to be married to Joseph, but before they came together, she was found to be with child through the Holy Spirit. 19 Because Joseph her husband was a righteous man and did not want to expose her to public disgrace, he had in mind to divorce her quietly. 20 But after he had considered this, an angel of the Lord appeared to him in a dream and said, "Joseph son of David, do not be afraid to take Mary home as your wife, because what is conceived in her is from the Holy Spirit. 21 She will give birth to a son, and you are to give him the name Jesus, because he will save his people from their sins." 22 All this took place to fulfill what the Lord had said through the prophet: 23 "The virgin will be with child and will give birth to a son, and they will call him Immanuel"--which means, "God with us." 24 When Joseph woke up, he did what the angel of the Lord had commanded him and took Mary home as his wife. 25 But he had no union with her until she gave birth to a son. And he gave him the name Jesus.

Chapter Two

The Visit of the Magi

1 After Jesus was born in Bethlehem in Judea, during the time of King Herod, Magi from the east came to Jerusalem 2 and asked, "Where is the one who has been born king of the Jews? We saw his star in the east and have come to worship him." 3 When King Herod heard this he was disturbed, and all Jerusalem with him. 4 When he had called together all the people's chief priests and teachers of the law, he asked them where the Christ was to be born. 5 "In Bethlehem in Judea," they replied, "for this is what the prophet has written: 6 " 'But you, Bethlehem, in the land of Judah, are by no means least among the rulers of Judah; for out of you will come a ruler who will be the shepherd of my people Israel.' " 7 Then Herod called the Magi secretly and found out from them the exact time the star had appeared. 8 He sent

them to Bethlehem and said, "Go and make a careful search for the child. As soon as you find him, report to me, so that I too may go and worship him." 9 After they had heard the king, they went on their way, and the star they had seen in the east went ahead of them until it stopped over the place where the child was. 10 When they saw the star, they were overjoyed. 11 On coming to the house, they saw the child with his mother Mary, and they bowed down and worshiped him. Then they opened their treasures and presented him with gifts of gold and of incense and of myrrh. 12 And having been warned in a dream not to go back to Herod, they returned to their country by another route.

The Escape to Egypt

13 When they had gone, an angel of the Lord appeared to Joseph in a dream. "Get up," he said, "take the child and his mother and escape to Egypt. Stay there until I tell you, for Herod is going to search for the child to kill him." 14 So he got up, took the child and his mother during the night and left for Egypt, 15 where he stayed until the death of Herod. And so was fulfilled what the Lord had said through the prophet: "Out of Egypt I called my son." 16 When Herod realized that he had been outwitted by the Magi, he was furious, and he gave orders to kill all the boys in Bethlehem and its vicinity who were two years old and under, in accordance with the time he

had learned from the Magi. 17 Then what was said through the prophet Jeremiah was fulfilled: 18 "A voice is heard in Ramah, weeping and great mourning, Rachel weeping for her children and refusing to be comforted, because they are no more."

The Return to Nazareth

19 After Herod died, an angel of the Lord appeared in a dream to Joseph in Egypt 20 and said, "Get up, take the child and his mother and go to the land of Israel, for those who were trying to take the child's life are dead." 21 So he got up, took the child and his mother and went to the land of Israel. 22 But when he heard that Archelaus was reigning in Judea in place of his father Herod, he was afraid to go there. Having been warned in a dream, he withdrew to the district of Galilee, 23 and he went and lived in a town called Nazareth. So was fulfilled what was said through the prophets: "He will be called a Nazarene."

Jim and Bonnie Inkster

3 THE SECOND DAY OF CHRISTMAS

The historic account, for it is not a fabrication of someone's imagination, starts in Matthew chapter one with 17 verses devoted to Jesus' genealogy. I mentioned previously how God takes insignificant people, calls up their potential and through faith they do the impossible. How wonderful is that? It is amazing to think I can impact my world for His sake.

I used to skip the genealogy because I found a list of names boring. But God is not into wasting space. There is a truth of His redemption story buried even within a genealogy. Jesus has significant figures in His family line: Abraham, Judah, David and Solomon. The father of our faith through to two of the best-known kings in history isn't a bad line-up. But if you look a little closer, you can find some people whose reputations you would not expect to find in the Savior's family tree.

How about Judah? The tribe that bears the hallmark of praise is fathered by a man who did not think it unwise to avail himself of the services of a prostitute along the side of the highway. Little did he know that she was his daughter-in-law? When it came to his attention that she was pregnant, he was ready to kill her. The problem was she had taken some of his personal effects, which she sent to him with the word that the owner of these is the father of my child. Judah admitted that she was more righteous than he in her actions. How would you like to have this situation occur in your church? One of your elders has impregnated his widowed daughter-in-law. How do you explain that?

Then there's Rahab, the prostitute, from Jericho. A prostitute? What's up with that? All our religious hackles go up with that thought. Her actions saved her and her whole family from destruction but also honored her with a descendant that redeems all who are evil. Then there's David, the murderer and adulterer. A great king who lived passionately in all that he did. Having lingered in Jerusalem when the army went to war, he used his position and authority abusively. Impregnating Bathsheeba, he then connives to have it appear that the child really is Uriah's by bringing him back from the front. Uriah out of concern for his fellow soldiers doesn't go to his wife. So David arranges through Joab to have Uriah ambushed by the enemy. After Uriah is dead he takes Bathsheeba as his wife and acts like nothing unusual has happened. Wow! This is a man whose heart is after God. It shows the deceptiveness of sin and the downward spiral of death it releases. The difference that set David apart from King Saul was his heart. When confronted by Nathan with his sin, he repented in fasting, sackcloth and ashes. He didn't care that the palace servants saw him. All he cared about was the mercy of God.

All these people are part of the family of our Lord. The church would like to sanitize this story. Would we hire someone with his family background to be our new pastor? The key to Jesus' family is the mercy and forgiveness of God. He was setting the backdrop for His redemption story. God forgives. He is not looking for vengeance upon us. He wants to have fellowship with us. Jesus said to his disciples in John 15:15 'I no longer call you servants, because a servant does not know his master's business. Instead, I have called you friends, for everything that I learned from my Father I have made known to you'. We are not only friends of God; we are sons of God through the work of Jesus' sacrifice.

The Christmas story is one of redemption. 'Jesus, being in very nature God, did not consider equality with God something to be grasped, but made himself nothing, taking the very nature of a servant, being made in human likeness. And being found in appearance as a man, he humbled himself and became obedient to death-- even death on a cross!' (Phil. 2: 6-8) Christmas is about gifts – the gift of life – so precious that only God himself could fulfill the part. This is what his genealogy is pointing to. See; see the hope and the future that only God can give. Our hope is sealed in His forgiveness, our future settled in His son. Thank you Lord for His birth.

4 THE THIRD DAY OF CHRISTMAS

"His mother, Mary, was pledged to be married to Joseph, but before they came together, she was found to be with child through the Holy Spirit." (Matthew 1:18) Pledged was betrothal, which meant that Mary in actuality was married to Joseph. At that time the betrothal was the first step of two in the marriage ceremony. It lasted a year during which time the groom prepared a place for his wife. When it was ready, he came for his bride and took her to his house.

Joseph had wed a virgin who before he could bring her to their new home became pregnant. The emotional pain and disappointment would have been crushing. This is not a casual relationship gone wrong. Because of the brevity of the scripture it is easy for a western person who is unfamiliar with this form of marriage to misinterpret the significance of this statement. From this point of view it seemed more of a business transaction, like purchasing a cow or a car, rather than a relationship of depth. Joseph would have known Mary before the marriage was arranged. He probably told his father that he liked her and would love to be her husband. Having arranged the marriage and entering into the betrothal period Joseph and Mary would have talked daily. I can imagine him showing her the progress he was making on their home. He would have given her gifts in preparation for the marriage. The anticipation of holding his wife in his arms intimately for the first time would have consumed his thoughts. Fear and desire equally daily companions as he labored toward the celebration of his wedding.

Marriage of a man and a woman is to be a beautiful picture of our Lord and us. Jesus said: "There are many rooms in my Father's home, and I am going to prepare a place for you. If this were not so, I would tell you plainly. When everything is ready, I will come and get you, so that you will always be with me where I am." (John 14: 2,3) While we wait for our lover to return we commune with Him through the Holy Spirit. We are not left alone. The marriage picture is one of faithfulness; I will never leave you nor forsake you.

To find his wife pregnant would have been devastating. The one he trusted, the one he loved, the one he worked daily for, the longing of his heart, had betrayed him with another man. I don't think Mary's story of an angelic visitation really held much credence with Joseph. Remember the Jewish people had not had a prophet in 400 years. It wasn't common to have angelic visitation or supernatural phenomena happening. She was pregnant and there was only one way that could happen. Sure the Holy Spirit came upon you and there you are a fulfillment of prophecy.

The word of the Lord came to Mary and in faith she believed and received. When the word of the Lord comes, we can embrace it, as did Mary, with faith, only to find it throws our whole world upside down. She probably never imagined while standing in the presence of Gabriel that Joseph would have thought of divorcing her. After all she loved him because he was a righteous man who cared for her.

The word of God always has an impact.

Jim and Bonnie Inkster

5 THE FOURTH DAY OF CHRISTMAS

"Because Joseph her husband was a righteous man and did not want to expose her to public disgrace, he had in mind to divorce her quietly." (Matthew 1:19)

It is important to note the most significant characteristic of the people involved in the most important event in human history. Zechariah and Elizabeth were upright in the sight of God, Mary was highly favored of God and Joseph was a righteous man. These were godly people who were blessed with the Lord's favor. Little did they know what that favor would do to their lives and place in the community.

Zechariah and Elizabeth had lived with the shame of barrenness for years. Now in their old age they were to have a baby. Elizabeth kept it secret for 6 months. She had faced the scorn and the whispering for years. Now, that which they had prayed for had happened and she wasn't about to let people mock God's answer to their prayers. Zechariah had lost hope and so lacked faith when he met Gabriel, the archangel. It seems almost severe to think God muted him for the entire pregnancy.

But our words are so powerful. "The tongue has the power of life and death, and those who love it will eat its fruit." (Proverbs 18:1) Our words can produce life and hope or death and despair. Both Elizabeth and Zechariah had to listen to the words of well meaning but thoughtless family and friends for years. They probably defended themselves by saying God would honor them with a child for He hears our prayers. The word says children are a gift from God and surely He would not withhold any good thing to those who love Him. Now Zachariah was unable to say one word of unbelief to his wife. She wisely did not expose herself to anyone else's words until the baby was well along. By this age both of them would be well aware of the power of others' words and the full effect of them on spirit, soul and body. Their shame would be lifted but they would still be the source of much gossip and speculation.

Mary, as I said previously, would not have thought that Joseph would have been so hurt. Joseph made the only decision that seemed reasonable to him under the circumstances. He did not want Mary to suffer any more public disgrace if he divorced her. He wanted to spare her as much of the shame as possible. But his life and hers would be the fodder for many an after dinner discussion. God's favor and plans for our life are sometimes contrary to the accepted wisdom and common sense of the world. People look at you like you are out of your mind when you are wholeheartedly following the Lord. These situations reveal what's in our heart. Not to God as He already knows but to us.

The text tells us that after Joseph considered this an angel of the Lord appeared to him in a dream. 'Consider' means to think carefully about something. It comes from a Latin root to examine. This gives us an idea that Joseph was contemplative, possibly analytical in his thinking. It also means he hadn't yet talked to Mary or anyone else. It is true that God knows our thoughts. What Joseph was considering was radical enough for God to take significant action to prevent the divorce. He sent an angel who told

Joseph that the baby truly was conceived of the Holy Spirit. He told Joseph that it was a boy and what his name was to be.

Joseph, then, took her to his home as his wife. His obedience fulfilled prophecy and showed how right his heart was before God. In fact throughout Jesus early years his father's obedience was crucial for the preservation of Jesus' life and the fulfillment of his destiny.

Joseph by his actions would have born the shame of Mary's pregnancy as well. In the eyes of the people in Nazareth his righteousness would have been questionable. But he feared God more than man and took the shame for the sake of a greater purpose. Sometimes when you are serving the Lord you can't explain to people what is happening. Obedience often creates an acceptable sacrifice that is only pleasing in our Lord's nostrils.

6 THE FIFTH DAY OF CHRISTMAS

Matthew 2:1-12 relates the visit of the magi or wise men. They had seen His star and followed it to find the future king. Herod was not happy with their appearance for their good news threatened him. To find where the Christ or Messiah would be born Herod went to the Pharisees and the scribes. Having queried when they first would have seen the star, he sent the wise men off to Bethlehem.

It is amazing to think that these men from the East could read the heavens well enough to travel all the way to Judea to visit the savior of all mankind. The book of Romans tells us that creation declares the reality of our creator. These men found him through creation. The reference material thinks that the Jews who were dispersed throughout the Roman world would have shared their expectation of a Messiah predisposing the gentile world to look for this coming king. It sounds plausible but, if you notice, neither the Pharisees nor their scribes were curious enough to go with these men to investigate what they had travelled so far to see. The Jews were disinclined to talk to gentiles if they could help it. If the Jews were that strongly sharing their faith in a Messiah, why didn't they go with them? Why didn't Herod?

The religious community, the very people He was coming to, weren't that tuned in. Herod is another case. He was threatened by the thought of another king arising in Judea. His kingdom was at stake. This is the very crux of the coming of Jesus. It isn't simply saving us from our sins but it is the kingdom of God overthrowing the kingdom of the prince of the air. The kingdom of darkness cannot prevail against this coming kingdom. It still can't if we walk in the kingdom of God.

Herod was not a righteous man. He was evil and dangerous. Matthew tells us that in verse 16 when Herod realized that the Magi had outwitted him, he was furious, and he gave orders to kill all the boys in Bethlehem and its vicinity who were two years old and under, in accordance with the time he had learned from the Magi. What evil lingered in his heart that he would do such a heinous thing? How can anyone in his or her right mind commit such an act? They can't, and he wasn't. His inspiration was from the same source that drove Judas to betray Jesus. Kingdom against kingdom! Jesus came to destroy the works of the evil one.

Jesus is the perfect sacrifice for all mankind. He came to the Jew but also to the Gentile. The angels announced his birth to the simple and humble shepherds. Blessed are the poor in spirit, for theirs is the kingdom of God. The rich Pharisees did not see the introduction to the kingdom of God. The poor did! Simeon and Anna as well as the shepherds! The Gentiles too saw the coming kingdom. They came and worshipped him with gifts of gold, frankincense and myrrh. Verse 10 says they were overjoyed, extremely happy. They gave richly by faith to a baby - seeing the king who would save not only Jew but Gentile too.

Then, being warned in a dream, verse 12, they went home another way. Somehow and in some way the church has come to think that God doesn't talk to non-Christians. He certainly does when it comes to the way of salvation. If He didn't, who would be saved? These men were very aware of the presence of the Almighty.

What a great reminder to all of us to be aware of the goodness of our God and not to forget what great things He has done for us, starting with the birth of His son!

7 THE SCRIPTURAL ACCOUNT ACCORDING TO LUKE

Chapter One

1 Many have undertaken to draw up an account of the things that have been fulfilled among us, 2 just as they were handed down to us by those who from the first were eyewitnesses and servants of the word. 3 Therefore, since I myself have carefully investigated everything from the beginning, it seemed good also to me to write an orderly account for you, most excellent Theophilus, 4 so that you may know the certainty of the things you have been taught.

The Birth of John the Baptist Foretold

5 In the time of Herod king of Judea there was a

priest named Zechariah, who belonged to the priestly division of Abijah; his wife Elizabeth was also a descendant of Aaron. 6 Both of them were upright in the sight of God, observing all the Lord's commandments and regulations blamelessly. 7 But they had no children, because Elizabeth was barren; and they were both well along in years. 8 Once when Zechariah's division was on duty and he was serving as priest before God, 9 he was chosen by lot, according to the custom of the priesthood, to go into the temple of the Lord and burn incense. 10 And when the time for the burning of incense came, all the assembled worshipers were praying outside. 11 Then an angel of the Lord appeared to him, standing at the right side of the altar of incense. 12 When Zechariah saw him, he was startled and was gripped with fear. 13 But the angel said to him: "Do not be afraid, Zechariah; your prayer has been heard. Your wife Elizabeth will bear you a son, and you are to give him the name John. 14 He will be a joy and delight to you, and many will rejoice because of his birth, 15 for he will be great in the sight of the Lord. He is never to take wine or other fermented drink, and he will be filled with the Holy Spirit even from birth. 16 Many of the people of Israel will he bring back to the Lord their God. 17 And he will go on before the Lord, in the spirit and power of Elijah, to turn the hearts of the fathers to their children and the disobedient to the wisdom of the righteous--to make ready a people prepared for the Lord." 18 Zechariah asked the angel,

"How can I be sure of this? I am an old man and my wife is well along in years." 19 The angel answered, "I am Gabriel. I stand in the presence of God, and I have been sent to speak to you and to tell you this good news. 20 And now you will be silent and not able to speak until the day this happens, because you did not believe my words, which will come true at their proper time." 21 Meanwhile, the people were waiting for Zechariah and wondering why he stayed so long in the temple. 22 When he came out, he could not speak to them. They realized he had seen a vision in the temple, for he kept making signs to them but remained unable to speak. 23 When his time of service was completed, he returned home. 24 After this his wife Elizabeth became pregnant and for five months remained in seclusion. 25 "The Lord has done this for me," she said. "In these days he has shown his favor and taken away my disgrace among the people."

The Birth of Jesus Foretold

26 In the sixth month, God sent the angel Gabriel to Nazareth, a town in Galilee, 27 to a virgin pledged to be married to a man named Joseph, a descendant of David. The virgin's name was Mary. 28 The angel went to her and said, "Greetings, you who are highly favored! The Lord is with you." 29 Mary was greatly troubled at his words and wondered what kind of greeting this might be. 30 But the angel said to her,

"Do not be afraid, Mary, you have found favor with God. 31 You will be with child and give birth to a son, and you are to give him the name Jesus. 32 He will be great and will be called the Son of the Most High. The Lord God will give him the throne of his father David, 33 and he will reign over the house of Jacob forever; his kingdom will never end." 34 "How will this be," Mary asked the angel, "since I am a virgin?" 35 The angel answered, "The Holy Spirit will come upon you, and the power of the Most High will overshadow you. So the holy one to be born will be called the Son of God. 36 Even Elizabeth your relative is going to have a child in her old age, and she who was said to be barren is in her sixth month. 37 For nothing is impossible with God." 38 "I am the Lord's servant," Mary answered. "May it be to me as you have said." Then the angel left her.

Mary Visits Elizabeth

39 At that time Mary got ready and hurried to a town in the hill country of Judea, 40 where she entered Zechariah's home and greeted Elizabeth. 41 When Elizabeth heard Mary's greeting, the baby leaped in her womb, and Elizabeth was filled with the Holy Spirit. 42 In a loud voice she exclaimed: "Blessed are you among women, and blessed is the child you will bear! 43 But why am I so favored, that the mother of my Lord should come to me? 44 As soon as the sound of your greeting reached my ears,

the baby in my womb leaped for joy. 45 Blessed is she who has believed that what the Lord has said to her will be accomplished!"

Mary's Song

46 And Mary said: "My soul glorifies the Lord 47 and my spirit rejoices in God my Savior, 48 for he has been mindful of the humble state of his servant. From now on all generations will call me blessed, 49 for the Mighty One has done great things for me-- holy is his name. 50 His mercy extends to those who fear him, from generation to generation. 51 He has performed mighty deeds with his arm; he has scattered those who are proud in their inmost thoughts. 52 He has brought down rulers from their thrones but has lifted up the humble. 53 He has filled the hungry with good things but has sent the rich away empty. 54 He has helped his servant Israel, remembering to be merciful 55 to Abraham and his descendants forever, even as he said to our fathers." 56 Mary stayed with Elizabeth for about three months and then returned home.

The Birth of John the Baptist

57 When it was time for Elizabeth to have her baby, she gave birth to a son. 58 Her neighbors and relatives heard that the Lord had shown her great mercy, and they shared her joy. 59 On the eighth day

they came to circumcise the child, and they were going to name him after his father Zechariah, 60 but his mother spoke up and said, "No! He is to be called John." 61 They said to her, "There is no one among your relatives who has that name." 62 Then they made signs to his father, to find out what he would like to name the child. 63 He asked for a writing tablet, and to everyone's astonishment he wrote, "His name is John." 64 Immediately his mouth was opened and his tongue was loosed, and he began to speak, praising God. 65 The neighbors were all filled with awe, and throughout the hill country of Judea people were talking about all these things. 66 Everyone who heard this wondered about it, asking, "What then is this child going to be?" For the Lord's hand was with him.

Zechariah's Song

67 His father Zechariah was filled with the Holy Spirit and prophesied: 68 "Praise be to the Lord, the God of Israel, because he has come and has redeemed his people. 69 He has raised up a horn of salvation for us in the house of his servant David 70 (as he said through his holy prophets of long ago), 71 salvation from our enemies and from the hand of all who hate us-- 72 to show mercy to our fathers and to remember his holy covenant, 73 the oath he swore to our father Abraham: 74 to rescue us from the hand of

our enemies, and to enable us to serve him without fear 75 in holiness and righteousness before him all our days. 76 And you, my child, will be called a prophet of the Most High; for you will go on before the Lord to prepare the way for him, 77 to give his people the knowledge of salvation through the forgiveness of their sins, 78 because of the tender mercy of our God, by which the rising sun will come to us from heaven 79 to shine on those living in darkness and in the shadow of death, to guide our feet into the path of peace." 80 And the child grew and became strong in spirit; and he lived in the desert until he appeared publicly to Israel.

Chapter Two

The Birth of Jesus

1 In those days Caesar Augustus issued a decree that a census should be taken of the entire Roman world. 2 (This was the first census that took place while Quirinius was governor of Syria.) 3 And everyone went to his own town to register. 4 So Joseph also went up from the town of Nazareth in Galilee to Judea, to Bethlehem the town of David, because he belonged to the house and line of David. 5 He went there to register with Mary, who was pledged to be married to him and was expecting a child. 6 While they were there, the time came for the baby to

be born, 7 and she gave birth to her firstborn, a son. She wrapped him in cloths and placed him in a manger, because there was no room for them in the inn.

The Shepherds and the Angels

8 And there were shepherds living out in the fields nearby, keeping watch over their flocks at night. 9 An angel of the Lord appeared to them, and the glory of the Lord shone around them, and they were terrified. 10 But the angel said to them, "Do not be afraid. I bring you good news of great joy that will be for all the people. 11 Today in the town of David a Savior has been born to you; he is Christ the Lord. 12 This will be a sign to you: You will find a baby wrapped in cloths and lying in a manger." 13 Suddenly a great company of the heavenly host appeared with the angel, praising God and saying, 14 "Glory to God in the highest, and on earth peace to men on whom his favor rests." 15 When the angels had left them and gone into heaven, the shepherds said to one another, "Let's go to Bethlehem and see this thing that has happened, which the Lord has told us about." 16 So they hurried off and found Mary and Joseph, and the baby, who was lying in the manger. 17 When they had seen him, they spread the word concerning what had been told them about this child, 18 and all who heard it were amazed at what the shepherds said to them. 19 But Mary treasured up all these things and pondered

them in her heart. 20 The shepherds returned, glorifying and praising God for all the things they had heard and seen, which were just as they had been told.

Jesus Presented in the Temple

21 On the eighth day, when it was time to circumcise him, he was named Jesus, the name the angel had given him before he had been conceived. 22 When the time of their purification according to the Law of Moses had been completed, Joseph and Mary took him to Jerusalem to present him to the Lord 23 (as it is written in the Law of the Lord, "Every firstborn male is to be consecrated to the Lord"), 24 and to offer a sacrifice in keeping with what is said in the Law of the Lord: "a pair of doves or two young pigeons." 25 Now there was a man in Jerusalem called Simeon, who was righteous and devout. He was waiting for the consolation of Israel, and the Holy Spirit was upon him. 26 It had been revealed to him by the Holy Spirit that he would not die before he had seen the Lord's Christ. 27 Moved by the Spirit, he went into the temple courts. When the parents brought in the child Jesus to do for him what the custom of the Law required, 28 Simeon took him in his arms and praised God, saying: 29 "Sovereign Lord, as you have promised, you now dismiss your servant in peace. 30 For my eyes have seen your salvation, 31 which you have prepared in the sight of all people, 32 a light for revelation to the

Gentiles and for glory to your people Israel." 33 The child's father and mother marveled at what was said about him. 34 Then Simeon blessed them and said to Mary, his mother: "This child is destined to cause the falling and rising of many in Israel, and to be a sign that will be spoken against, 35 so that the thoughts of many hearts will be revealed. And a sword will pierce your own soul too." 36 There was also a prophetess, Anna, the daughter of Phanuel, of the tribe of Asher. She was very old; she had lived with her husband seven years after her marriage, 37 and then was a widow until she was eighty-four. She never left the temple but worshiped night and day, fasting and praying. 38 Coming up to them at that very moment, she gave thanks to God and spoke about the child to all who were looking forward to the redemption of Jerusalem. 39 When Joseph and Mary had done everything required by the Law of the Lord, they returned to Galilee to their own town of Nazareth. 40 And the child grew and became strong; he was filled with wisdom, and the grace of God was upon him.

The Boy Jesus at the Temple

41 Every year his parents went to Jerusalem for the Feast of the Passover. 42 When he was twelve years old, they went up to the Feast, according to the custom. 43 After the Feast was over, while his parents were returning home, the boy Jesus stayed behind in Jerusalem, but they were unaware of it. 44 Thinking

he was in their company, they traveled on for a day. Then they began looking for him among their relatives and friends. 45 When they did not find him, they went back to Jerusalem to look for him. 46 After three days they found him in the temple courts, sitting among the teachers, listening to them and asking them questions. 47 Everyone who heard him was amazed at his understanding and his answers. 48 When his parents saw him, they were astonished. His mother said to him, "Son, why have you treated us like this? Your father and I have been anxiously searching for you." 49 "Why were you searching for me?" he asked. "Didn't you know I had to be in my Father's house?" 50 But they did not understand what he was saying to them. 51 Then he went down to Nazareth with them and was obedient to them. But his mother treasured all these things in her heart. 52 And Jesus grew in wisdom and stature, and in favor with God and men.

Jim and Bonnie Inkster

8 THE SIXTH DAY OF CHRISTMAS

From Mary's perspective in Luke

Before we can delve into the birth of Christ and Mary's part in it we need to have a look at the one who would prepare the way for the Lord. The birth of John the Baptist is woven into the birth of Christ, not because it's an interesting event, but because he would fulfill a role that would begin to prepare people for the unusual.

Luke tells us that Zechariah was a priest and Elizabeth was also from the priestly heritage of Aaron. They were both upright and blameless in the sight of God, yet even though at this time they were "well along in years", they had no children.

In those days to be barren was considered a curse. People would have looked at Elizabeth and would have thought 'tut-tut". You must have done something that was very displeasing to God. They would have been carrying the shame and the disappointments of unfulfilled hopes and dreams for a long time. I would think the expectation of ever having a child would be long passed.

This can happen to us all in various ways. We have an expectation of what we would like to have happen. We might have it all planned out and somehow the dream is lost. It could be anything from a relationship, a business adventure, exam marks, or to having or not having children. There are countless disappointments that come our way. There are a few things we need to make very clear.

God was not punishing Zechariah and Elizabeth. Luke (1:6) very clearly states that they were walking rightly before God. God, however, in His wisdom was waiting for the proper or right time. There is a timing of God that often seem late to us. We may be hanging on with what we feel is our fingernails. But….

God's ways are not our ways. Psalm 34 says lean not unto your own understanding. You only see a part of the picture but God sees the whole. He is bringing people together with events that will shape history – His Story.

And that was the way it was with Zechariah and Elizabeth. He wanted to bring about the beginning of the invasion of the Kingdom of God in a miraculous way. The whole region, in fact all of Israel, would have been talking about this birth. The people knew that she was barren and she was old. She would have been the talk of the town. They knew that Zechariah had a divine visitation and couldn't speak. This was a very unusual event.

All the people would have been wondering and watching. God has prepared the events for this strategic moment. John was to prepare a people for the Lord. This was all part of preparing the people even before he was born. God was already beginning to till the soil of Israel's heart.

God is good. Even though at times we don't

understand what's going on He is still in control and He is good. Romans chapter 8 and verse 28 says, "He works all things together for good for them that love the Lord."

9 THE SEVENTH DAY OF CHRISTMAS

Zechariah was going about his priestly duties in the same manner he had always done. Much like you on any ordinary day. The alarm goes off, you roll out of bed, into the shower, get dressed and ready to go. You stop at Starbucks for a latte before you head for the office where you will turn on your computer and hear those 3 lovely words, "You've got mail!"

The interesting thing is that Zechariah drew the straw so he got the privilege of going into the temple of God to burn incense. At this exact time the people gathered to pray. Why? Our prayers are like incense that goes up before our Father in heaven. Prayers are like a sweet-smelling aroma to him as they reach His ears. We see in Revelation 5:8 that the incense is the prayers of the saints. Then in Revelation 8:3-5 that the angels add 'much' incense to the prayers of the saints and this smoke goes up before the Lord.

You see, you and I offer up our frail prayers but God takes that which we offer and He adds the punch to them! You may feel like your prayers are hitting the roof and bouncing back. But I assure you they are going into that golden bowl to which incense is being added to make them ascend to the Lord. How exciting!

So, on this day that seemed like any other day, Zechariah is mirroring 'on earth as it is in heaven' and an angel shows up! Zechariah sees him and is filled with fear. I'll bet he was! Think about it, you are going about your day and suddenly standing beside your desk at the office is an angel. This angel came with a purpose and that was to deliver a message.

The first thing he tells him is "don't be afraid" (too late! Already trembling!). His prayers have been heard. This is so reassuring. We need to know that our prayers are being heard. They don't just go up into the 'cosmic realms" and float in a void. They land somewhere – on the Father's ears! We need to be assured of this: God hears and answers prayer. He is a rewarder of those that seek Him. This is where faith comes in. Without faith it is impossible to please God. You come to Him, you believe that He is, that He actually exists and is interested in all the details of your life. Check Hebrews 11 verse 6.

Now, the angel begins to prophesy to him or deliver the message from God. He says first your wife is Elizabeth. I like this detail – I am sure that Zechariah knew who his wife was but somehow this validates what he is about to say. I was with Jim in San Diego and my mom was taking care of our twins. I was desperately trying to get a hold of her to see how things were going. We were at the pay phone (no mobile phones in those days) and this man came up to us. He said your mother is on the phone to her sister and the twins were both doing well. He then said the Lord also told him to tell us that we would have another child. It would be a son and then he prophesied into his future. I started to laugh because at that point I had the alpha and omega, the beginning and the end, and was not even considering having another child. It took several years for me to be willing and we had 2 more children. The first of them to be born was a son. The fact that God took the time to confirm all the other information to me eventually opened my heart to receive healing from the trauma of the late stages of pregnancy and the birth of the twins.

The angel goes on to say the child she will bear is to be called John. This was a bone of contention with the relatives because no one had this name before. But names are significant and the name, John, means 'precede'. The verb, precede, is to go ahead of, in front of as in rank, sequence or time. John needed to precede Jesus as he was given the task of going on before the Lord to make a people ready for the Lord.

John would be filled with the Holy Spirit from birth, going in the Spirit and in the power of Elijah. He would bring many people back to the Lord, winning the hearts of the fathers to their children and the disobedient to the wisdom of the righteous.

John is a type of New Testament believer. We need to be filled with the Holy Spirit and work in power. God will use us to prepare the people to meet the King. He will use the foolish to confound the wise. John didn't look the part of the religious but he caught the hearts of the people.

Let us be the ones that act with the authenticity of our convictions. In this way the world will see something powerful displayed as we allow the King to turn the hearts of the fathers to the children and the hearts of the children to their fathers. Let the spirit of Elijah come!

Jim and Bonnie Inkster

Jim and Bonnie Inkster

10 THE EIGHTH DAY OF CHRISTMAS

Mary was a young woman who was in the waiting stage between betrothal and the actual wedding celebration. She would have had all the anticipation, expectation and dreams of any one of us looking forward to that "special" day.

Right in the midst of the waiting Mary had an unexpected visitor – an angel! His first words to Mary were: "Greetings, you who are highly favored? The Lord is with you." This greatly troubled her, as it would you! That's like picking up the phone and someone saying you have been chosen for a prize or your name has been picked for jury duty. But favor sounds good - promising! Who wouldn't want to be favored by God?

The angel goes on to inform her what the favor of God will mean to her. She would be the mother of a son, not just any son, but the Son of the Most High. Mary's question at this time is a very human question. I remember getting prophetic words and thinking this very thing. "How can this be?" It is a human response to a super natural God. We think on one plane - the natural one. The angel, Gabriel, makes this statement: "Nothing is impossible with God!"

What a great statement! How easy it is for us to forget that God is in control of ALL THINGS. Our tendency is to look at things with our natural eye and say it can't happen. How easy it is for us to loose perspective. I love flying; jet travel makes the globe so accessible. But at one time the thought of flying was beyond man's thinking – now it is normal.

One thing flying does is change perspective. Up in the sky looking down on the world things below look so small. For God to intervene in our lives is a small thing for him. What seems like a mountain is nothing from His heavenly perspective. He is interested in all the details of our lives and nothing is impossible for Him to do.

The question is: do we believe it? Do we believe that He will use us to change the world? Do we believe that He is watching over His word to perform it? Isaiah 55 says: Do we believe that there is really nothing - that is no thing, God cannot do? Have we put Him in a box and confined Him to our thinking?

The challenge is this. If Gabriel came to you or if God asked you to do something would your mind stay "greatly troubled", or would you take hold of the Spirit of God and allow Him to work His work in you? You never know how the unexpected will come into the midst of your normal day.

Jim and Bonnie Inkster

11 THE NINTH DAY OF CHRISTMAS

"I am the Lord's servant," Mary answered. "May it be to me as you have said". What a fantastic response from such a young woman. Mary didn't hesitate to say "Yes, Lord". I am sure she didn't have it all worked out in her head but what she and Abraham, the father of the faith, have in common is that they believed God without knowing details.

There are two attributes required to be the Lord's servant that we can glean from Mary, willingness and faith.

1. Willingness: Mary says yes to the call of God for her life. She has no idea what that is going to look like, where it will take her or the

sorrow that she would encounter because of it. However, she is willing to trust that her God knows what He is doing and that He is able to keep her.

In I Chronicles 28:9 David is saying to Solomon to acknowledge God, serve Him with wholehearted devotion and with a willing mind. This word, willing, means to be acquiescent, to incline, or to volunteer. Acquiescent means to agree by not objecting, to yield and submit. How many times do you hear children arguing with their parents instead of being willing to do what has been asked? How may times have I not been willing? David asks in Psalm 5 that the Lord would grant him a willing spirit to sustain him.

Abraham like Mary was told to leave his country, his people and his father's household and go to a land that the Lord would show him. And so Abram left. He was willing to go, willing to respond to the voice of God. Abram also had …

2. Faith: God told Abram that he would become a great nation and be blessed. That

he would have offspring as many as the stars. In Genesis 15:6 it says that Abram believed the Lord and He credited it to him as righteousness.

In the same way Mary believed what the angel said. Mary was not just willing but responded in faith, believing that if God said it, then He can and will do it. You can be willing but you must have faith to believe that God can do all things.

Faith is a key ingredient in being the Lord's servant. Faith is the currency of heaven! Without it Hebrews 11 says it is impossible to please Him! With faith you can conquer kingdoms, administer justice and gain what is promised!

Mary believed the promise brought to her by Gabriel. But, she was also willing to submit to whatever that would look like in her life. In being the Lord's servant she became the woman to give birth to the Son of God. From that point on all generations have called her blessed!

Jim and Bonnie Inkster

12 THE TENTH DAY OF CHRISTMAS

After Mary's encounter with Gabriel she hurried off to compare notes with her cousin, Elizabeth. Elizabeth and Mary are decades apart in age and yet they have each experienced a supernatural event.

It is worth noting that to experience the awesomeness of God is not restricted to age. The Lord says to Jeremiah not to despise his youth and don't say "but I am only a child". On the other hand Moses was 80 when the call of God came to him and he led the largest congregation of people in history. We are never too young or too old to allow His kingdom to come and work in and through us.

Notice as well that these two were women. God's call

on your life is not hindered by your gender. Jeremiah 1 says that before you were formed in the womb I knew you. God was not surprised when you were born by your gender, color, nationality or the place you live! Our times are in His Hands and He has called each of us to fulfill a unique destiny for His purpose.

Elizabeth confirmed the call of God on Mary's life when she walked in the door for even John leapt in her womb at just the sound of her voice. I can see Mary and Elizabeth jumping around, holding hands and excitedly proclaiming the wonders of their great God! What an exciting time it would have been seeing Elizabeth six months pregnant just like the angel said!

The call of God was on these women and on the offspring they were carrying. Elizabeth would give birth to John who would be the last prophet of the Old Testament. Mary being the younger would be the woman to give birth to the One that would bring the New Covenant into being.

Both John and Jesus had a purpose. John came to prepare the way of the Lord. The hearts of the people were hard and he was preparing them – turning the soil of their hearts to receive the One to come. Jesus also had a purpose and that was to destroy the works of the evil one. He did that by bringing the Kingdom of God to the people.

Each of us has a call and a destiny to fulfill. You won't be the mother of Jesus – the Savior of the world. But you could be the mother or teacher, Sunday school teacher, friend or pastor of someone who through knowing you has a supernatural encounter with God and goes on to do great exploits. We all have a purpose and a destiny to fulfill.

Jim and Bonnie Inkster

13 THE ELEVENTH DAY OF CHRISTMAS

Mary's Song

"Mary's Song" as it is referred to is a delight to read. She is full of the joy of the Lord and her mouth is the overflowing expression of her heart. For out of the abundance of the heart the mouth speaks, and her mouth was filled with reverence and gratitude for the Lord.

There is a word that is used twice in this song and that is humble. In verse 48 Mary says the Lord remembers her humble or lowly state and again in verse 52 that he has lifted up the humble. This word, humble, refers to the condition of having no or little money also a place of being unpretentious and unassuming. Jesus himself chose to be born to a humble or lowly family. Why would that be? Peter and James say that God resists the proud but gives grace to the humble. This is not referring to the circumstances of life but to the heart.

Jesus himself teaches us that if we humble ourselves or change and become like a child then we will enter the Kingdom of Heaven. In fact we will be considered the greatest in the Kingdom. Matt 23 says that whoever humbles himself will be exalted. Jesus did not choose to be born into a wealthy family or a family of position. Isaiah 57:14 -15 says to build a road and remove the obstacles for the people. Why? Even though the Lord lives on a high and holy place He also abides with him who is contrite (that is repentant) and humble in Spirit.

Jesus wants to live in us. He wants us to have the Kingdom of God express itself through us. He was a living example of how we do that. We do that by being humble in heart. He will revive the spirit of the humble – He will pour out His grace upon your life if you stay in that position that says I need you Lord.

John the Baptist kept saying repent for the Kingdom of God is at hand. We need to change our way of thinking. That is what repent is – a changing of the mind. He was removing the obstacles out of the way, that is our pride. God wants to come to a humble and contrite people and revive us and lift us up.

Jim and Bonnie Inkster

14 THE TWELFTH DAY OF CHRISTMAS

The Foolish Thing

God chose the foolish things of the world to shame the wise; God chose the weak things of the world to shame the strong. He chose the lowly things of this world and the despised things – and the things that are not – to nullify the things that are. (I Corinthians 1:27) From a human point of view to have the King of Kings being born to young inexperienced parents is not wise. To have her conceive out of wedlock – shameful – then to have her travel on the back of a donkey from the security and comfort of her own home – just ridiculous!

But God's ways are not our ways and in His perfect plan He had Mary in the final stages of pregnancy when Caesar Augustus called for a census. This meant a 70 - 80 mile trek for Joseph and Mary to the town of Bethlehem. If it had been me, I am sure the question in my mind would have been "why now?"

There are so many events or timings of God that we might consider coincidental but the Great Conductor is ordering our footsteps aright. Jesus needed to be born in Bethlehem to fulfill prophecy. The Lord just uses man and natural events to fulfill his purposes. He does the same in our lives. At just the right time He brings people into our lives that can speak a word in season or have us at a place that will touch our lives forever.

For Mary and Joseph to make the journey to Bethlehem is one thing but then to find nowhere to stay must have been heartbreaking and frustrating. These people are known for their hospitality. It wasn't unusual to welcome a stranger into their home. To be rejected or turned away from where they expected a welcome was a prophetic sign of what the Savior would encounter later. The very people that He comes to will often turn Him away at the door of their heart.

Fortunately there was a barn that had room to welcome the tired couple. Not exactly the sterile and clean environment that we like to have our babies born into. But this too is a prophetic statement as to where the Savior would come. It is right in the midst of life's situations, problems, sickness, addictions and needs that God loves to come. Jesus is not waiting for us to "clean up our acts" before He comes in. If that were the case we would have no need for a Savior. He wants us to welcome Him into the midst of whatever is happening in our lives so that His power in us can work in and through us.

If I had been Mary I would have had many questions about the timing of the birth and the place. But God in His wisdom was proclaiming to the world a profound statement. "I have chosen the foolish things, the shameful things, the despised things, the lowly things to confound the wise and nullify the things that are so that no one may boost before Him."

ABOUT THE AUTHORS

Jim and Bonnie Inkster have been married for 40+ years at the time of publication. They have had the joy of raising four children together. Their family is their abiding passion, ever expanding to now include nine grandchildren.

Jim and Bonnie Inkster lived in Canada until 1999 when they moved with their two youngest children to England. They have been educators as well as church leaders. In 2000 they started a leadership training college in Essex, subsequently planting churches in London and Birmingham as well as praying in 30+ nations. They love to teach and train people to reach their potential and to truly enjoy life. January of 2013 saw them re-locate to Kelowna, BC.

They speak at seminars and conferences worldwide. They conduct seminars on marriage, parenting, leadership and a host of other topics.

OTHER BOOKS AND RESOURCES BY JIM AND BONNIE INKSTER

24 Secrets To Great Parenting
(paperback)

Jim and Bonnie share from their vast experience the principles that helped them raise four great children. It is written in a light-hearted, easy reading style perfect for the busy parent with very little spare time on their hands.

Available through Amazon and on Kindle.

8 Questions Every Parent Wants Answered (DVD)

Jim and Bonnie surveyed hundreds of parents to find what issues are their greatest concern regarding their children. Eight questions were consistent from parents throughout the world.

These questions have been addressed in a powerful and entertaining format. Each session takes less than 10 minutes with great ideas for successful application within your family.

Available through Amazon.

OTHER BOOKS AND RESOURCES BY JIM AND BONNIE INKSTER

24 Secrets to Great Parenting
(audiobook)

Jim and Bonnie felt that this great book had to be available to everyone including those who don't like to read. The research shows men prefer to listen, women prefer to read.

Jim was professionally studio recorded reading this charming and helpful book. Great for in the car or on your personal player when exercising or simply chilling.

Great Blogs @ www.jimandbonnie.co.uk

Jim and Bonnie write a weekly blog giving thoughtful and sometimes witty insights into relationships, marriage and parenting.

Don't miss it!

OTHER BOOKS AND RESOURCES BY JIM INKSTER

Eyes of Wonder
(paperback)

Eyes of Wonder is a delightful collection of life experiences with the children and grandchildren that have taught Jim everything he needed to know to be an adult.

Similar to the Chicken Soup for the Soul series this gives you simple downhome wisdom. Always good for a chuckle too!

Available through Amazon and on Kindle.

The Heart of the Matter
(paperback)

The Heart of the Matter is an interesting journey into the heart of God and our response to His amazing unconditional giving. It reveals excellent revelation and insight into the heart of our heavenly Father.

Available through Amazon and Kindle

Great Blogs

www.gatewaysministries.com

www.jimandbonnieinkster.com

Jim and Bonnie can be contacted through these websites.

Jim and Bonnie Inkster

www.ingramcontent.com/pod-product-compliance
Lightning Source LLC
Chambersburg PA
CBHW031606040426
42452CB00006B/424